Virtuous Heart

Twelve Buddhist Stories to Awaken and Inspire

Leza Lowitz

Art by Amanda Giacomini

These simple, beautifully written and illustrated folk tales, based on stories from the Pali scriptures, are among some of the oldest recorded stories in the world. If you are not already familiar with them—as I wasn't—I promise you will find them delightful. While charming in their own right, they also embody everyday wisdom (the Buddha reportedly used them to illustrate his teachings) that will inspire all of us, of any age or spiritual background, to endeavor to become our best selves.

—Nina Zolotow, co-author of *Yoga for Healthy Aging: A Guide to Lifelong Well-Being* and Editor-in-Chief of the "Yoga for Healthy Aging" blog

VIRTUOUS HEART will make you remember the wisdom of animals with very human lessons you'll never forget. So powerful, resonant and needed today!

—Jennifer Pastiloff, author of *On Being Human: A Memoir of Waking Up, Living Real, and Listening Hard*

In this evocative retelling of these classic Buddhist morality tales, each fable starts with the relatable, all-too-human cravings of the villain—a twist that makes all the more touching the transformations wrought by the compassion of the awakened animal teachers. Pairing Leza Lowitz's deft prose with the delicate brushstrokes of Amanda Giacomini's illustrations, these stories are tuned to delight seekers of all ages.

—Anne Cushman, author of *The Mama Sutra: A Story of Love, Loss, and the Path of Motherhood*

Virtuous Heart: Twelve Buddhist Stories to Awaken and Inspire published by Wandering Mind Books/KDP, 2019.

Text © Leza Lowitz, 2019
Art © Amanda Giacomini, 2019
Book Design © Amy Perich 2019

*   *   *

ARTIST ACKNOWLEDGEMENTS:
I would like to thank my family for being my inspiration and modelling the virtues to me on a daily basis. In particular, I would like to thank my mother for her courage, my father for his wisdom, my sister for her compassion, and my husband, Nicholas, and the Giacominis, for their loving kindness.

AUTHOR ACKNOWLEDGEMENTS:
Firstly, I would like to thank Amanda for inviting me on this beautiful journey. It has been a blessing to be a part of it. Huge gratitude to my mother, Donna Mendelsohn, who is the embodiment of wisdom, generosity, and selfless kindness. Thanks also to my father, who generously supported this book. I owe a particular debt of gratitude to poet Jane Hirshfield, to whom I expressed doubt about my ability to retell these classic stories, and questioned the need to do so. Hirshfield, who had translated the ancient Japanese court poets Onono Komachi and Izumi Shikibu for modern times, encouraged me, saying that every generation needs its own renderings of the classics. Gratitude as well to my husband Shogo for embodying the wisdom of these teachings in word and deed, without fail. I would also like to thank my son for being a great teacher, and all of my beloved pets for embodying unconditional love and kindness.

The author and artist would like to gratefully acknowledge all of their teachers—past, present, future—and family, friends and community who supported them on this journey.

Table of Contents

Foreword

In 2006, I made a pilgrimage to visit the ancient site of the Ajanta caves in central India. These two-thousand-year-old caves were carved by hand into the side of a cliff. As the artisans carved out thirty three caves, they created the most exquisite sculptures and reliefs of Buddhas, Bodhisattvas, and the like, then the caves were painted floor to ceiling with narrative tales not only from the Buddha's life but of his many past lives.

It was in these caves that I first saw the mural of a thousand Buddhas sitting together, which launched me into a twelve-year journey of painting Buddhas all around the world. To date I have painted over 15,000 Buddhas in over 15 states in 5 countries. Visiting the caves not only inspired my 10,000 Buddhas mission but I also discovered a collection of ancient wisdom embodied in the Jataka Tales, or Tales of the Past Lives of the Buddha.

In these stories, the Buddha incarnates in hundreds of different forms, many of which are enlightened animals. In each story, he accrues some spiritual merit, through the practice of kindness, compassion, courage, patience, loyalty, and honesty. For me, a meditator for over thirty years and a yogi for twenty five, these stories spoke to me about what spiritual practice is all about.

That year, I asked my dear friend Leza Lowitz if she could re-write some of the Jataka tales so that I could illustrate them and we could bring these teachings to a new audience of modern yogis and spiritual seekers.

When I read her versions of the Jataka tales I wept with joy. They opened my heart and allowed the dharma to land softly inside. Her sensitive voice, the voice of a poet and a deep practitioner of yoga and meditation, brought forth the magic of these stories. Each one is uplifting and inspiring and carries with it Buddha's teaching of how we all have the ability to spiritually evolve, we all have the potential to become enlightened. The enlightened animals in the stories show us the way and every opportunity we have to choose patience over anger, kindness over vengeance, we get one step closer.

In the twelve years since she first drafted this collection, I have had the opportunity to travel and teach to tens of thousands of yogis around the world at festivals, conferences, and workshops. Often, when I teach at these events I share the versions of the Jataka tales that Leza wrote. I have witnessed first-hand over and over again how students can easily absorb these beautiful teachings through the stories. I see their eyes filling with tears and I know the dharma had landed in their hearts. While there are many versions of the Jataka tales available, nothing moves my heart the way Leza's versions do. After every class I am always asked: where can I get these stories? I am so thrilled that Leza has made these stories available in *Virtuous Heart*, the collection that you have before you now.

As an artist, my hope is to capture the spirit of these enlightened animals. I want to communicate their light and the radiance of their beings. I used oil paints in thin layers to create depth, and sanded and varnished the images so they feel ancient and timeless like the stories. Leza and I are honored to have you join us on this journey to celebrate the wisdom, power, and beauty of sentient beings everywhere, in all their forms.

Amanda Giacomini
Summer, 2019

Introduction

The Jataka tales are 2,500-year-old Pali scriptures based on the lives of the Buddha before he became awakened. These 550 ancient tales are among the oldest recorded stories in the world, set mainly in the animal kingdom to offer humans lessons in how to live morally and ethically.

These gentle creatures illustrate the laws of karma: cause and effect. The Buddha reportedly used these stories to spread his teachings, and monks compiled them during the Ashoka era. The folktales eventually made their way across Asia, reaching Tibet, Burma, China, Mongolia and Japan. In the West, they might have been the basis for *Aesop's Fables* and Chaucer's *Canterbury Tales*. Many native cultures around the world cherish animal gods for their wisdom. The concept of animals as holy beings, messengers of divine wisdom, and embodiments of unconditional love is universal and time-less.

Amanda Giacomini's 2006 trip to India inspired the creation of this book. She traveled to Ajanta, a UNESCO World Heritage Site 200 miles north of Bombay, where vibrant paintings of the Jataka tales are etched into the walls of meditation caves nestled deep in a ravine.

"The only way to describe Ajanta is 'epic,'" she wrote to her friends (including me). "Walking through the 2,000-year-old hand-carved caves was like being transported back in time. The murals that cover the walls depicted the past lives of the Buddha and were like a dream. I had studied these images for the past year as the subject matter of my art, but seeing them in person was so exciting it made me want to cry." Amanda's love of animals inspired her to continue painting these epic creatures, and she asked me to retell the Jataka tales to accompany her paintings.

Inspired by Amanda's renderings of the grace, strength, and vulnerability of these beautiful animals, I set about selecting my favorites from the tales. Hundreds of versions exist today, told in different styles and settings, but I wanted to strip the stories to their moral imperative. What is the essence of the ethical choice each protagonist faces? From a Buddhist perspective, what is the correct choice on the path? Sometimes the Buddha makes a misstep. This is part of the path, too. The path of learning, of wisdom, of discernment.

I took the unusual step of starting with the villain's desire. What does the villain, our shadow side, want? What lengths would he go to in order to achieve the goal? After all, this desire (or attachment) is the motivation that leads him to the action that will force him to confront an ethical dilemma. The outcome will determine his fate. In almost each tale, the Buddha, incarnated as an animal or element of nature, shows him the Right Way. Every time, the Right Way is found in helping others. This lesson is all the more powerful in our culture and mindset of "me, me, me" and "every man for himself." Look where this has gotten us. We would do well to reconsider this approach. Time is running out for our species and our precious planet. A virtuous heart of selfless compassion is what is needed to foster peace and tolerance in the world.

And not just for humans.

In today's world, animals are used as commodities and consumed by humans for their skins, bones, and flesh. They are abused and enslaved for entertainment. They are kept as pets in all manner of circumstances, making an enormous and choiceness sacrifice for human beings. We wanted to honor their enormous sacrifice. What if they really are Buddhas? Would we treat them differently? In these retellings, I wanted to celebrate the joy and love they give us as part of the human family. I also wanted to celebrate that most generous of all forces—the sun, which gives and gives, never asking for anything in return.

According to the laws of karma, everything we do, say, or even think plants seeds that grow in our lifetime or carry over into a future incarnation. The understanding is that you can't have a bad outcome from a good seed, just as you can't plant a bean and sprout a banana bush. What we do comes back to us. The Jataka tales remind us of this simple and powerful lesson, lived over lifetimes.

As "The Wisdom of Animals" noted, "Animals don't set out to teach humans anything at all, but we all have a lot to learn from our interactions with them.... Time around animals invites us into a world in which most of the things that obsess us have no significance – which corrects our characteristic over-investment in matters which make only a limited contribution to the essential task of existence: to be kind, to make the most of our talents, to love and to appreciate."

Indeed. These twelve tales of the patient ox, the compassionate snake, the selfless sun, and others are ancient, but the virtues of devotion, kindness, honesty, generosity, patience, bravery, and self-sacrifice are as urgent as ever. In our fractured world, where empathy and listening have given way to anger, factionalization, and argumentation, these lessons in what it means to be living peaceably and with compassion could not be more important. Just as the Buddha used these tales to entertain and teach, it is our hope that students and teachers of mindfulness and yoga can share them to uplift and inspire today. As Jack Kornfield says: "Stories often help people see how the very difficulties they encounter become the places that the heart grows wiser and more full of compassion."

May the tales in *Virtuous Heart* awaken the soft heart within all of us that longs for truth, beauty, love, and connection. May we remember these gifts and share them with others.

Leza Lowitz
Summer, 2019

My name is the Buddha, The Awakened One. I live high up in the clouds. And in your heart, when you remember to invoke me.

Thousands of years ago, I came down to earth and taught humanity how to live in peace. Over the years, I have watched from afar as people forgot how to do this.

I returned to earth to remind them, disguising myself as animals and other beings to teach kindness, courage, patience, compassion, loyalty, gratitude, and love.

These are the beatings of a virtuous heart. Place your hand on your heart and come walk with me.

CHAPTER 1

The Devoted Elephant

"I WANT RECOGNITION," thought the hunter as he wandered through the mountains one afternoon, lost in thoughts of fame and fortune. So taken was he with these daydreams that by the time night fell, he'd lost his way completely. Suddenly, a beautiful white elephant appeared and, humbly letting the man ride on his enormous back, returned him to the holy city.

But the hunter, far from being grateful, decided to go back to the forest to capture the elephant and bring him to his beloved king.

"Finally, I can get the recognition I deserve!" he gloated.

Unaware of the danger he would soon face, the elephant lovingly tended to his blind mother, gathering food for her and pouring water over her head with his trunk. His greatest joy was giving her food and drink, showering her with love and devotion. When the hunter and his men returned to capture the great white elephant, he peacefully allowed himself to be taken without force. With tears in his eyes, he said goodbye to his beloved mother and was brought to the king.

The king had never seen such a magnificent creature, but the elephant, far from being happy, couldn't contain his grief. Though the king placed every kind of delicious food in front of him, the white elephant refused to eat.

The king was indignant. "This is the best food in all the land! How dare you refuse my hospitality!" But the elephant still couldn't eat a bite. Finally, weak from hunger, he confessed. "How can I enjoy such a feast when my blind mother cannot eat? She will starve without me, so I, too, will starve without her."

Moved by the elephant's devotion, the king released his captive and returned him to the mountains, where the elephant had a joyful reunion with his mother, who indeed was thin and weak. Eating the delicious food from the castle that her son had brought, she soon regained her health, and the two lived in peace and happiness from then on.

Recognizing that devotion and sacrifice are stronger than fame or fortune, the hunter asked the elephant for forgiveness. The great white elephant gently bowed his enormous head and accepted, and the two remained friends for life.

CHAPTER 2

The Selfless Deer

"I WANT RICHES," thought the fisherman as he held his rod over the river. He'd caught as many fish as he could and was planning to sell them for the highest price. But his basket became so full with fish that he lost his balance and tumbled into the water. The rushing current carried him swiftly downriver.

"I'm drowning! Please save me!" he called out, trying desperately to keep his head above water as he was thrown against the rocks and boulders along the riverbank.

A beautiful golden deer made her home by the river. Hearing the man's cries, she rushed to pull him out. He quickly revived and, stunned by her beauty, asked what he could do to repay her for her kindness.

"I don't need payment. I merely want to live in peace and solitude," she said and requested only that the fisherman promise not to tell anyone where she lived. Thankful to her for saving his life, he quickly agreed.

But the fisherman soon forgot all about his promise. The beauty and radiance of the golden deer were legendary, and the king had long desired to capture her. Blinded by greed, the fisherman proudly revealed the whereabouts of this magnificent creature, receiving a generous reward for the information.

The king set out with his hunters to find the golden deer. The fisherman took them to the spot where she had saved him, and they hid in the brush until they caught a glimpse of her shimmering form as she darted gracefully through the trees.

Gasping at her beauty, the king took out his bow and arrow. Just as he pulled back the string and took aim, the deer spoke.

"Please wait! I saved this man's life," she said softly.

The king gasped again. Her voice was that of an angel.

"He promised not to reveal my existence," she continued, "And he has betrayed me. If I must go with you, please take me alive." She dropped to her knees.

"Is this true?" the king asked and turned to the fisherman.

"Yes, your highness," the fisherman admitted. One could not lie to a king, after all.

"Betrayal is a crime of the highest order!" the king decreed. "I will have to kill you!" He ordered his huntsmen to draw their bows at the fisherman instead.

"I have a wife and many children. How will they live?" the fisherman pleaded. Seeing the pitiful man overcome with fear, the golden deer asked the king to spare his life.

"Kill me instead," she said. "I live alone in the forest, and if I die, no one else will be harmed."

Moved by her generosity, the king let the fisherman go. He recognized the deer as a great teacher of compassion, generosity, and self-sacrifice, and he set her free. She was never captured again.

CHAPTER 3

The Kind Monkey

"I WANT THE BEST, AND I WANT ALL OF IT!" thought the king as he bit into the luscious yellow fruit. "What is this magnificent fruit, and where did you get it?" he asked his subjects.

"Why sir, it is a mango. We found it in the river. It must have fallen from a tree in the forest, and floated down to our village...."

The king waved his hand impatiently. "Bring me all of them, and now!"

"Of course, your highness," the vassal replied. He gathered his men, who gathered their shovels and hatchets. Soon they made their way into the forest to uproot all the mango trees in order to plant them on the palace grounds. The king was so happy about the prospect that he decided to follow along for the ride.

The king's men didn't think at all about the monkeys who lived in the mango trees. But all the monkeys could think of was saving the beloved mango grove where they had lived for hundreds of years. The trees were like houses and villages all in one. Those trees were the only homes they had known!

When the men began to dig out the trees, the monkeys resisted with all their might, wrapping their arms, legs, and tails around the trunks. Mangoes fell by the hundreds, only to be quickly scooped up by the king's men. The monkeys screeched and jumped, trying to scare them off, but they were outnumbered.

"What's all the commotion?" the king asked as he arrived with his servants.

Not wanting to disappoint him, the vassal ordered his men to pull out their hatchets and chase the monkeys straight to a cliff.

The monkeys were cornered. Another mountain stood beyond the cliff, but it was too far away for them to jump safely. Suddenly, a grand monkey emerged from the crowd, stepping up to the cliff. The monkey king! Having seen how bravely his men had fought to save their trees, he stretched his arms to the mountain and grabbed onto a rock with his fingers. Then he stretched his legs into the forest and held onto a branch with his toes.

"Hurry now! Use my body as a bridge and go quickly!" he ordered his men.

But they hesitated, not wanting to step on their beloved king's back.

"I command you," he bellowed. "Do it now!"

With tears in their eyes, the monkeys scampered across the bridge that their beloved leader had made with his body. They tried to step lightly, but there were so many of them moving so quickly that before long their king was wounded and bleeding.

The human king emerged from the forest to behold the remarkable sight. "Who are you and what are you doing?"

"I'm the monkey king," the proud savior answered, even as the monkeys continued to run over him to safety.

"And you let your subjects trample you like that?"

The monkey answered without hesitation. "They've given their lives in service to me. They'll die if I don't help them now. They planted and grew that mango grove to feed me. Do you think my one life is worth more than their thousands?"

The human king suddenly felt deeply ashamed. It was his desire for the luscious mango, after all, that had led to this tragedy.

"Stop!" he called out to his men. "Let them go. I have enough." He ordered them to put down their shovels and hatchets.

Then he promised not to dig up any more trees. "I deeply apologize," he said. "Please forgive me. Let your monkeys come home. I won't harm them or their trees."

The monkey king nodded quietly and let his people walk over him again as they returned home.

When the last monkey had returned, the human king gathered his men and sat them down in a circle in front of the monkey king. He pointed at all the trees they had already uprooted and at the carts overflowing with mangoes.

"Beside this fruit, I have the even greater treasure of your loyalty, which until now I failed to see. Many of you have served me for years, and I owe you everything. But what have I ever given you that can compare to what this king has given his people?"

Following the monkey's example, he bowed low to the ground, honoring his men.

They were deeply moved. Tears fell from their eyes.

"We love you like a father," they said.

"And you like my sons," he replied.

Then he turned to the monkey king. "I promise to respect the mango groves and never harm them again." He asked his men to replant the trees they'd uprooted.

"No, please." The monkey king held up his paw. "It's too late for that. Instead, why don't you plant them in your men's honor at your palace and share the fruit with anyone who wishes it—rich or poor, beggar or saint?"

The king agreed. Then the two kings bowed deeply to each other, and a peace was made between them.

Though he was battered and bruised, the monkey king's wounds healed, and he fully recovered.

From then on, there were enough mangoes for both monkeys and humans alike, and the two kingdoms coexisted peacefully in the mountains and forests, rivers and valleys for generations to come.

CHAPTER 4

The Forgiving Fish

"WE WANT WATER," said the villagers, carrying buckets in each hand as they walked to the lake. They filled their washbasins and pitchers to overflowing, and then came back for more. It was Tuesday, washday, and the villagers washed their clothes and their bodies, their gardens and their chariots. Every week, they did this, not noticing the rains had stopped and the huge lake was all but dry.

But the fish who lived in the lake noticed and were helpless to stop the villagers' wasteful ways. Gasping for breath, they twisted and turned on their sides, desperately trying to cover themselves with the life-giving liquid the villagers had squandered.

The fish elders called an emergency council. Each day for a hundred days they prayed for rain or that the villagers' jars and buckets would break, but nothing happened. Then one day, the sky opened up and thunderclouds burst and the rain poured down. The villagers were overjoyed, and the fish danced a spiraling rain dance to thank the rain gods for heeding their prayers.

But the rain didn't stop. There was so much that the lake filled and filled and the villagers' buckets overflowed and their fields and terraces flooded like rivers, drowning their crops.

As desperate to save themselves as the fish had once been, the villagers gathered around the lake and summoned the fish elders.

"Please help us! Can't you call the rain gods back and have them stop this downpour?" they begged.

With a heavy heart, the wise queen fish listened to their plight. "You stole our water, and many of us were lost. Now, you want us to help you?"

"We didn't realize what we had done!" the villagers shouted.

"Now you know." The queen fish was fierce.

"Our crops are ruined. We'll surely starve if this flooding continues!" the villagers cried.

They still think only of themselves.... the queen fish thought. How could she help them?

"This lake is a mirror," she said, "so look into it and learn."

Then she spun on her tail and dove back into the

water. It pained her heart to do this, but she knew that humans were a greedy and thick-headed bunch.

If the lesson wasn't hard, it wouldn't be learned.

The only way to teach them the value of life was to take away their food supply just as they had taken away the fish's water.

Two days went by. The deluge continued. Finally, the villagers returned and called on the queen fish to surface.

She rose majestically and listened patiently to their words.

"Queen dear, we now understand. Without food, we can't live. Without water, *you* couldn't live."

The queen fish nodded.

"We understand that our greed caused you great suffering. We can never repay you, but at least, please accept our apology. We understand how precious water is and promise never to abuse it again."

The queen fish smiled and accepted the apology.

"Let us live together and share our water, air, and earth as one family," she said. And with a festive slap of her tail, she called the other elders to council.

They gathered in a swirling circle underwater and sent a powerful prayer to the rain gods to stop their offerings. The queen fish was delighted to see the villagers gathered in a circle on land, dancing to the rain gods, too.

"One family!" the villagers shouted gleefully. "The lake is our mirror."

Before long, the rains stopped, and the earth soon regained its balance. And from then on, rain fell when it was needed, and the villagers took only what they needed, nothing more, and nothing less.

And the fish danced and swirled in their lake, and the villagers danced and swirled on the ground, all together under the luminous bright light of the moon.

CHAPTER 5

The Silent Turtle

"I WANT EVERYONE TO KNOW HOW BRILLIANT I AM," said the king, who gathered his subjects from far and wide, sat them down in his courtyard, and babbled on about this and that.

His main area of expertise was the colors of the rainbow. He loved to collect specimens from nature to show off the many hues of the spectrum, as if he himself had created them!

But his repetitive and vain words were soon forgotten. When his show-and-tell hour was over, people would return to their homes, happily shutting the doors and sitting by the fire, telling each other thrilling tales of wise animals and beneficent Buddhas instead.

One day, while the king was boring his subjects, far away in the countryside, a little turtle was floating in his pond when two geese flew overhead. As they passed, they admired his stunning jade green shell, and they were so grateful for its brilliance that they decided to share with him the beauty of the world that they saw from high above.

"Why don't you ditch this mud puddle and come see the world?" they said, and told the turtle of the marvelous land teeming with glorious vistas—sunlit plains and snowy peaks like ornaments and jewels.

The turtle looked around. His pond, too, was teeming with ornaments and jewels—the finest brown sticks and the richest green moss. "No thank you, I'm perfectly content here," he replied, sunning himself in his favorite swampy corner.

But the geese wanted not only to share the world with him but to spend more time looking at his luminous green shell. They were very convincing.

"Oh, silly little turtle, don't you want to fly? You can't stay forever stuck on land, can you? Don't you want to tell your grandchildren how you were the first turtle ever to soar in the clouds, like a bird?"

"How would I fly?" the turtle asked, intrigued. He knew he shouldn't be swayed, but the thought of flying weightlessly in the sky was just too tempting for words.

"Well, you wouldn't fly, exactly," they backtracked. "We'll fly you. You see, both of us will hold the ends of a stick in our beaks, and you'll hold it in the middle, with your mouth, and then off we'll go. We'll bring you back the same way you came. We promise!"

The turtle mulled it over. It did make sense. "Okay, just this once."

"Great! But you mustn't open your mouth. Otherwise, you'll fall."

"Easy," said the turtle. And off they went.

They flew over rivers, valleys, and forests, great deserts and splendid mountains, and the turtle silently enjoyed the glories of the earth. But when they passed above the castle where the king was droning on and on about the color indigo, the little turtle gasped in awe at the crowds. He'd never seen so many people.

And then he realized that he was falling. By opening his mouth, he'd let go of the stick, and he tumbled towards the earth.

If he barely escaped death, it was only because the quick-thinking court jester saw the brilliant green shell falling and had the foresight to throw down his cape and command the people in the crowd to hold the edges. In this way, they caught the poor turtle.

Seeing this, the two geese flew off in fright, fearful that the king's hunters would notice them.

The royal retinue quickly gathered around the shining green stone, for the turtle now appeared to be nothing more than a stone. Scared out of his mind, he'd tucked his head, tail and feet back into his shell.

"My, my, my. What have we here? A flying turtle?" the king exclaimed, puffing out his robes. "I've never seen such an exquisite shade of green, a rare gem of emerald, known to exist only in the far reaches of the Western swamps, I dare say... How on earth did you get here? What remarkable striations you have, those amazing indentations, and...."

The turtle tried to reply, but he could barely get a word in edgewise.

"You must be a magical being. This is an omen," the king continued. "An offering from the gods. How did you get here? I've never seen such an amazing creature as a flying turtle. So, tell me, tell me!" the king demanded.

Again, the turtle tried to talk, but the king blathered on.

Finally, the turtle rolled onto its back so that the king couldn't see his magnificent shell anymore.

"Can I speak now, your majesty?" asked the turtle, whose voice was, naturally, muffled by the ground.

"Of course!" the king said and chattered on while the turtle righted himself.

"I opened my mouth!" said the turtle.

For once, the king was speechless.

"What do you mean?"

The turtle sat calmly as he told the story of flying with the birds, and how he hadn't been able to keep his mouth shut as he promised, and how opening his mouth almost cost him his life.

When the turtle was done speaking, you could have

heard a pin drop in the courtyard. The crowd waited for the king's pronouncement, but for once there was only silence.

Beautiful, golden silence.

Seeing the Buddha before him, the king vowed never to engage in useless speech again. And from that day on, the turtle was consulted whenever an important decision had to be reached. Each time, he required a little silence and calm to help the king choose his words carefully and wisely.

CHAPTER 6

The Patient Ox

"I WANT TO BOTHER HIM," thought the monkey as he spied a huge ox standing quietly in the shade of a banyan tree, minding his own business. After all, there is nothing more enticing to a mischievous monkey than a boring old ox.

So the monkey hopped right on top of the ox's back, but the ox didn't even flinch. Then the monkey jumped up and down, but the ox only swayed gently, as if a feather had landed on him.

Ever so annoyed, the monkey took a stick and began to tap on the ox's legs, but again the ox didn't seem bothered at all. He merely swayed from side to side, as if riding a gentle ocean wave.

More determined than ever to rile the ox, the monkey scratched the ox's ears with his stick, but again the ox was unfazed. Beginning to become enraged, the monkey pulled on the ox's tail, but received no response. So he hurled handfuls of grass, hay, dirt, and finally pebbles at the ox, who didn't even seem to notice.

Exhausted, the monkey crumpled into a heap at the ox's feet and demanded an explanation.

"Mister Ox, why didn't I bother you? I tried all my best tricks to annoy you, but nothing worked."

The ox merely smiled.

At this, the monkey was even more perplexed. Perhaps the ox didn't know its own strength. Was that it? The monkey decided to spell it out for the placid creature. "Your huge body could smother me. Your hooves could crush me. Your horns could wound me in an instant. In fact, you could defeat any warrior in the realm, and yet you do nothing and let me torment you. Why?"

"Why should I bother to harm you?" the ox said softly. "You harm yourself quite enough."

"I beg your pardon?" the monkey asked, outraged. No one talked to him like that.

"Nature has already given you such a small mind that you are your own worst enemy. Why make you suffer more?"

At this, the monkey stopped in his tracks. Perhaps this thick old ox wasn't as dumb as he looked, the monkey thought.

"Causing others pain brings me no happiness. Nor does it you, I see," the ox said without malice.

At those words, the monkey woke up, as if cold water had been splashed on his face.

The ox was right. In fact, all that bullying had made him miserable. And he hadn't even succeeded in annoying the ox at all. So he bowed to the ox and asked him to be his teacher.

Humbly, the ox accepted.

"Come stand by me," he said, and the monkey did as he was told.

"Patience," explained the ox, "is the greatest weapon of all."

The monkey nodded, waiting for more wisdom. "Simply stand under this banyan tree, and enjoy the shelter of its leaves," the ox whispered gently.

The monkey did so, and it was divine.

"Now enjoy the solidity of the earth under your feet, and the coolness of the breeze through your fur, and the sun streaming on your back, and the warm feeling in your heart."

The monkey closed his eyes and did as his teacher instructed. He stood very still, and after a while, he was able to feel what his teacher felt. He no longer wanted to harm anyone. He wanted only to feel this kind of peace and let others feel it as well. Tears fell from the monkey's eyes. The ox wiped them away.

The two of them stayed there for a very long time, just quietly feeling.

And for the first time in his life, the monkey was really, truly happy.

CHAPTER 7

The Loyal Swan

"I WANT SUCH BEAUTY ALL FOR MYSELF," said the nobleman upon hearing the legend of the golden swan who lived high up in the mountains.

The nobleman's desire to possess the luminous swan was so great that he ordered his workers to build a lotus pond more beautiful than any before, so that all the swans in the world would come to swim in it.

Word of the magnificent pond soon reached the swan and his loyal retainer. One day, the two set out to see the site for themselves. Sixty thousand swans accompanied their leader on this glorious excursion, anticipating a wonderful day basking under the sun in the magnificent pond with its sacred lotus flowers.

The crafty nobleman hid behind some bushes and watched the procession arrive. He waited until the two swans floated to the middle of the pond, then released his trap. With a snap, the golden swan's foot was caught, and he let out a cry of surprise.

Panicked, the sixty thousand swans quickly flew away, leaving the retainer alone by his master's side.

"Why don't you go, too? You're not caught, so fly away to freedom." The nobleman waved his hands at the swan's retainer, urging him to go.

But the retainer refused to leave his master's side. "What freedom is it to live without devotion? There would be no greater prison than to abandon my master," he said, looking up at the golden swan lovingly. "Take me, too. I will gladly stay if only to be by his side."

Astounded by the servant's willingness to sacrifice even his own life for his master, the nobleman suddenly understood that there was a much higher power than possession—that of loyalty and honor.

At that realization, he decided to set both swans free, celebrating them with a sumptuous feast and a promise never to capture another creature ever again.

CHAPTER 8

The Brave Horse

"I WANT TO PROTECT MY LAND," declared the king, looking over the beautiful country that was the richest and happiest in all the world.

The long-standing peace his people had enjoyed was the result of years of cooperation between the king and the villagers, who shared everything they had.

But recently the peace had been threatened by kings from other lands who were jealous of the peaceful king's popularity. They banded together and decided to overthrow him, for this is the nature of power—those who don't have it want it, and those who have it want to hold onto it, and get more of it.

One by one, the leaders of the neighboring countries lined up to challenge the peaceful king and take away his territory. They were seven in number, and each had a large and powerful army of devoted warriors ready to fight at any time. An attack was imminent, but the peaceful king struggled with the decision. He had to protect his land and his people, but he didn't want to go to war.

The peaceful king sat down in a field next to his trusty black stallion and suddenly began to cry.

You can imagine the horse's surprise, as kings never cry!

"Please, control yourself!" the horse begged his master.

"Seven kings and seven strong armies! Surely we don't have the strength to go up against them all," the king fretted. "We will be ruined. I should give myself up."

"Not to worry," the brave horse assured him. "Your kingdom is my heart, and I'll gladly give all my strength for peace in this land. I am strong, and can fight any warrior and win."

"But surely you'll die!"

The horse shook his head. "Gentle king, you have given me everything I need, and it is my duty to fight for you and protect you, so I will gladly go to battle. With your love in my bones, there is no power greater. So lend me your best knights and we'll win each time. For your children, and their children, and their children's children."

The king stroked the majestic horse, who was like a son to him. Through his hands, he transmitted his own kind power to the animal, and blessed him with strength and bravery.

The horse bowed and received the king's power and blessings. Then he let himself be suited up in a splendid armor. The king's best knights gathered and went off to battle, with the brave horse leading the way.

The first battle was fought and won—not without hardship, but still, a victory was secured. The second battle went so, and the third, too. Six battles were fought in this way, and all were won. The kings of six countries were captured and brought to the peaceful king's court.

But on the seventh battle, the brave horse was wounded, and walked with much difficulty back to the castle, where he lay broken and dying at the king's feet.

"Victory is yours," the horse said. "I have done my best for your honor."

The king's eyes flowed with tears of gratitude. "How can I repay you?" he asked, bowing low to the black horse's side.

"Behold these seven kings before you," said the horse, his voice quivering with pain.

The king gazed at the seven leaders, bound in chains. The once powerful men looked pitiful and frightened.

"Do not kill them or imprison them. Let them go, and let them pledge to you to become peaceful warriors in the neighboring countries, protecting you and each other from the North, South, East and West. Come together as one for the future, and fight no more wars."

"Yes, your majesty," the king said, because he understood that it was really the horse who was the king, and he the mere subject. He owed his life, his power, and his land to the bravery of this horse. And he was humbled and awed.

The king granted the royal horse his final wish, and the brave horse died in his arms.

From then on the eight kingdoms lived with peace among men and animals, and the legend of the brave horse and the eight wise kings endured for hundreds of years.

CHAPTER 9

The Compassionate Snake

"I WANT TO SURVIVE," thought the farmer as he surveyed his meager fields. The crops were poor, as they had been every year.

What to do? The farmer sat down under a fig tree and rubbed his head. The earth was fertile, the rains were adequate, the sun was plentiful, and still, his crops didn't thrive. "How shall I feed my family?" he wondered aloud. "How will I give my son a better future than the life I now have?"

Just then, some twigs fell from the tree and landed by the farmer's side. He looked up and was surprised to see a beautiful serpent wrapped around a branch. The farmer rose, startled. The serpent puffed up its hood and reared back, ready to strike.

"Please sir, don't harm me," said the farmer. "I meant only to seek a better view of my land."

"Your land?" the serpent hissed, obviously disagreeing. "You humans have such nerve! To think that just because you have feet, the earth you walk upon belongs to you!"

The farmer's eyes grew wide with worry, and he recoiled, moving away from the snake. But the snake didn't bother to harm him. It merely slithered into the higher branches of the tree and out of sight.

The farmer considered what the snake had said. Perhaps the creature had a point. This was not his land after all. Before he himself was born, the animals had lived there. And this place—why, it had been the serpent's hallowed grounds! There had even been a shrine to the serpent god here years before. All at once, the farmer understood. He had not granted the land's owner the proper respect. From that day on, he vowed to honor the serpent and the land.

So the next day he brought a basket with fruit, coconut cake, and the sweetest milk, laying them out at the base of the tree. He decorated the basket with fragrant flowers and said a prayer to the snake, bowing deeply at the foot of the tree. He even lit myrrh incense, fanning its fragrant smoke out between the leaves.

The next day, his crops looked healthier than ever, so the farmer repeated his ritual. Each day, he made an offering to the snake and to the earth, and each day, his crops flourished. And what is more, sparkling red rubies began to appear at the base of the tree! He almost thought to gather them up, but then told himself that this was the serpent's tree and he should above all respect what was not his.

One day, he had to go to the capital for business, and he sent his son to the fields instead, instructing him on the important ritual that would guarantee the success of the crops.

After plunking the basket down, the boy mumbled his salutations and then, seeing the rubies, took them and began to search in vain for their source. The serpent did not slide down the tree, and the boy left.

When the son returned the next day, he saw that the offering had not been touched. Instead of leaving the new basket, he ate its fruit and drank the milk himself, and put the flower in his lapel. The snake watched from above, clicking his tongue. Hearing the noise, the boy began to shake the tree. The snake lost his balance, and his tail dropped over the branch. The boy seized it and pulled the snake to the ground.

"Ungrateful slug! Why didn't you accept my offering?" he demanded, pinching the snake's tail between his fingers.

"Your offering was not from your heart," the snake told him.

"Take this from my heart!" the boy said and aimed a rock at the serpent's head.

But being quick when he needed to, the snake lunged and bit the boy's arm.

Soon after he'd staggered back to the village, the boy fell ill. The snake's poison coursed through his body, and when his father returned from the capital that night, he found his son clinging to life, barely able to breathe.

The farmer went into the fields, only to find his crops destroyed.

He called out to the snake. "What have you done to my only son?"

"Go away!" the snake said from his tree.

"Please, lord snake. Have mercy on me!"

"You came only for the rubies."

Seeing that the basket's offerings were untouched and that the rubies were gone, the farmer understood.

"Please let me apologize for my son. He is a greedy boy, and it was my mistake to entrust him with such an important job."

"Is that so?" the snake said, unimpressed.

"Please accept my apology," the farmer again begged.

"Even if I never give you a single ruby?"

The farmer nodded.

"Even if your crops die again?"

Again, the father nodded. "My son is worth more than a million rubies or the best crops in the world. Please tell me how to take the poison from his body. If you do so, I will never come here again."

"Hmmmm...." the snake replied, considering. These humans were truly a difficult sort. But seeing that the farmer spoke the truth, the snake instructed him to make a compress of herbs and to place it on the wound for a fortnight. The compress would suck the venom out, and the boy would return to health.

"Thank you, thank you!" The farmer got down on his knees. "I will bring you offerings every day for the rest of my life, I promise."

"But how will you survive? Your crops will surely die."

"I will go to the capital and find work there. I will send money back to my wife and son. I'm not so old yet. I can still work...."

The snake sat on his branch, wondering at the folly of humans. The man was indeed old, and the snake wondered how long his body would hold out against the hard work of farming. But the father and son were different, he saw, and this made him smile.

As the farmer walked off, the snake called out, "Tell your son that he is old enough to work the fields. If he makes an offering with a pure intention, then the crops will thrive."

"Thank you. I will do so. I promise," the farmer vowed.

When he returned home, the farmer made the compress just as the snake had instructed, and his son soon regained health. From then on, the boy made his offerings with a pure intention, as he was genuinely grateful to the snake for saving his life. And he learned to work the fields, and his love of his work grew stronger and stronger with each passing day, like the flourishing crops that rose from the land.

So moved had the merciful snake been by the father's loyalty that he decided to bless the fields and make every seed planted there grow hearty and strong.

CHAPTER 10

The Sorry Sun

"I WANT TO SATISFY MYSELF TO THE FULLEST," thought Brother Sun as he and Sister Moon set off for a distant galaxy to visit their grandparents, Thunder and Lightning.

Dressed in their finest garments, they journeyed through the night, leaving behind their father, the North Star. Their mother, West Wind, had taken ill, so their father was staying home to tend to her.

In the far-away land, their grandparents treated them to a marvelous sound and light show, full of drama and music—cymbals and crashing, flashing and strobe. Then Brother Sun and Sister Moon enjoyed a sumptuous feast of heavenly morsels that only grandmas can prepare, made especially for them.

Brother Sun devoured everything he could reach and licked his rays with pleasure. Sister Moon ate daintily, tucking choice morsels under her beams for her parents who waited in the distant galaxy with nothing so spectacular to eat.

When it was time to go, Brother Sun and Sister Moon set off into the night. As they neared home, their father welcomed them by opening his arms wide and shining a luminous path.

"Did you have a good time, my children? Did you eat to your heart's content?" he asked.

"Thank you, papa. It was wonderful," said the Sun, whose belly was round and full. "I thoroughly enjoyed myself!"

"And how about you, dear Moon?" the North Star asked, looking to his daughter.

"Indeed, it was, as brother said, fantastic. I wish you and mother could have joined us. But since you couldn't, I brought you some of grandma's special treats." Sister Moon lifted her beams and spread the food on a platter, then gave it to her father.

The North Star bowed and brought the tray to West Wind's room. He was patient and kind, and did not seem upset. But mother, who was really the Buddha and not long for this world, couldn't hide her disappointment.

"Did I raise my son to be so selfish?" she asked, tears falling down her cheeks.

"Perhaps so," father said sadly.

"Did I teach him to think only of himself?" she wept.

"There, there, darling," Father North Star consoled her, but it was no use.

"I don't have much strength left, but if it's the last thing I do, I am going to rid him of his selfishness," she vowed and summoned her power. She left her bed, and before Brother Sun could speak in his own defense, she raged, casting a strong spell on him.

"Mother! What have you done?" Sister Moon said.

"Nothing he wouldn't have done to himself," her mother replied wisely. "I'll only help him learn his lesson more quickly. It will be less painful this way." Then she smiled wistfully to herself, because sometimes the Buddha is wrathful and fierce, the better to teach the more stubborn amongst us, the better to bring our shadows to light.

She told her son that his rays would be forever red hot, scorching and burning everything he touched for himself—including his own body.

But if he thought of helping others when he shone, everything he shed his light on would grow instead, and he would be mostly comfortable and at ease. That way he would have to think of others and be gentle with them, unless he wanted to spend the rest of his days alone, baked in the most subtle pain.

"As for you, lovely daughter, you will be cool and radiant, magical and mysterious. You will reflect your brother's light more gently, reminding him of his better self. And if he falters, you will cover him completely, and darken his light."

"But mother...." Sister Moon wept. The thought of hurting her brother pained her immensely, even if it was to help him.

"Now, now," West Wind said, and with that, she swept herself up into the heavens and was gone.

When Brother Sun reached out to touch his sister, sparks shot out from his fingers. He quickly recoiled. Had he only reached out to her to console himself? Did he consider for a minute what she was feeling, no longer free to come and go as she pleased? He shook his fists at the sky, cursing his mother, his father, his fate. He screamed and cried, kicked and stomped until there was nothing left to do but collapse in tears.

After many days of crying, a sudden clarity filled his heart. Turning his gaze inward, he saw that he hadn't been the easiest son. He'd been hot-headed, unpredictable, and rebellious, prone to igniting wildfires, scorching continents, and setting off meteoric disturbances without the slightest provocation. Maybe that's why West Wind had been so hard on him, he now realized. He'd wreaked great havoc for fun and never thought twice about it. And to his sister? What had he done but tease and bully, mock and frighten her ever since they were young?

He turned to his sister with compassion. After all, though she had done nothing wrong herself, she had been punished for his misdeed. And their mother had passed onto the heavens far sooner than they had expected, perhaps of a broken heart.

"I'm so sorry, sister," he said, sending out the brightest light from his heart to hers, watching it radiate onto her silvery orb. She backed away and shimmered faintly in the distance, then flickered and faded. Her twilight seemed to have suffered enormously from the strain.

"Accept my apology," Brother Sun pleaded to his sister, "It's all I have left."

Then he turned his gaze heavenward.

"I'm sorry I hurt you mother," he said. And he really, truly was.

"Even though you're no longer here, I'll try to think more of others from now on in your honor," he promised.

And from then on he did, sending out his bright rays, everything they touched flourishing and growing. Sister Moon soon forgave her brother, regaining her luminosity. When her brother rested, she cast a path of moonbeams over all the land.

That is how the fates of the Sun and the Moon became tied together—one hot, one cool, one in the light, one in the dark, forever linked to their mother and father, whom they were never again to forget.

For years to come, both Brother Sun and Sister Moon shone their distinctive lights out over the universe, even when father North Star went quietly up to join their mother in the sky.

CHAPTER 11

The Generous Pigs

"I WANT TO BE HAPPY FOREVER," the little pig told the big pig each night before they went to bed, as they thought of all the wonderful things they had done that day and filled their hearts with gratitude.

They lived with an old woman, a weaver who loved them and cared for them as if they were human. She had found them as piglets, abandoned in the mountains, and had carried them home in her basket.

Every day, she fed them buckets of grain and even let them sleep in the house when it rained. They grew bigger and bigger, happier and happier.

But the woman grew old and frail, and was unable to feed herself. She couldn't carry on working as a weaver, and soon, men from the village came to the house and offered to buy the pigs. There was a big wedding planned in the village, and a feast was to be prepared.

"I can't give you those pigs. They're my children!" she said.

But the men stayed for hours and convinced her, and she finally relented, agreeing to sell the larger one, but only after a day to say farewell. That night, she let the pigs sleep in the house, even though it wasn't raining.

The next morning, she called the little pig to the kitchen. The pig grew afraid, as he knew the old woman always called the bigger pig first. Something wasn't right.

The little pig ran back into the barn and hid. When the big pig called out her name and finally found her, the little pig confessed her fear.

"I'm scared," she said. "First those men, and now this. And it didn't even rain last night! Something isn't right!"

Her friend took a deep breath and put his hand on her back. "It's okay," he said. "Follow me, and we'll be all right."

With that, he marched straight to the house, straight to where the villagers were waiting with a rope and a sack.

"Wait! Don't go there! They'll kill you," the little pig wailed.

But the big pig just sighed. "I know, my friend. In fact, I've known this for a long time. That is why we were fed such good food and cared for so well."

"Why didn't you tell me?" she asked, trembling.

"What good would that have done? It would only have made you worried. And we had such fun together, didn't we? Slopping around in the mud, rolling in the fields, and who could forget those hay fights?!"

The little pig sobbed. "Don't go.... Please. I'll be so lonely without you!"

"Don't cry for me, friend. My whole life has led me to this moment. I must go bravely and offer myself so that this woman, who has cared for me so deeply, can live."

With tears in his eyes, he bid the little pig farewell.

"I'll go with you, then!" she said and hung a garland of roses around her friend's neck.

And he gathered some roses from the garden and did the same for her.

And so, holding hands, they walked into the house and came right to the villagers' ropes, and went willingly into their sacks, making a game of it, telling each other stories that they were going to the most beautiful place in the world, a sacred mountain where they would be happy together forever, playing and laughing, snorting and shouting, rolling and running free. Like they had done as children, a long, long time ago.

And when they were let out of the sacks at the wedding party, the crowd gasped in awe.

For instead of two pigs, before them were two radiant angels with garlands around their necks and love pouring from their hearts.

When the bride saw the love the angelic pigs shared for each other, she asked her beloved to give her the best wedding gift of all. Because he loved his wife dearly, the groom agreed.

And so the villagers spared the two pigs their lives, setting them free into the mountains, where they lived to be old and frail themselves, and where all they had imagined came true.

CHAPTER 12

A Thousand
Different Forms

"I WANT POWER," thought Maha. He was a yogi who had great physical and psychic strength and could put his body in amazing postures—even folding his limbs together so tightly that he disappeared.

One day, he came upon a festival where a magic competition was being held, and he performed his tricks to win a golden bowl, though the Buddha had forbidden yogis to use their powers in this way.

Maha wasn't alone in rejecting the Buddha's prohibition. Many doubted the rule, and a group of these yogis gathered and decided to challenge the Buddha. They believed that he had forbidden magic because he himself actually had no powers.

"Sometimes generosity and kindness are not enough to quell the doubters," the Buddha mused. So, grudgingly, he decided to use one of the many skills he had gained during his years of yogic study. With it, he would perform what others would see as a "miracle."

It wasn't that he wanted to prove his own superhuman powers. Rather, the Buddha sincerely wished for people to benefit from the wisdom and beauty of his teachings, which they could not do if they doubted him.

So he traveled to the town of Shravasti to accept the challenge.

Drawing all of his energy into his heart, he stood at the center of the hundreds of people gathered in the town square. He divided his own body into a thousand replications and filled the crowd with exact images of himself.

"Look around! What do you see?" the Buddha asked the stunned skeptics.

When they turned, they were indeed amazed. Every one of them stood next to a Buddha!

Maha, in the midst of the crowd, was amazed at his teacher's skill.

"I can use my powers," the Buddha said, looking directly at his student, "but what use are they if nothing good comes of them?"

All at once, Maha understood. He took the beautiful golden bowl that he had won and gave it to the poor villagers, who were then able to buy enough food to live for years and years.

Seeing this, the naysayers reconsidered. They no longer doubted the Buddha's powers and were even more taken by his humility. But it was the generosity he had inspired in his once-greedy student that impressed them most of all. It was one thing to change yourself. But to inspire others to become better people?

This truly was magic.

About the Author

LEZA LOWITZ is a writer and yoga teacher. She grew up in Berkeley, received her B.A. in English Lit from U.C. Berkeley, and M.A. in Creative Writing from San Francisco State University, and moved to Japan. She owns a popular yoga studio in Tokyo, Sun and Moon Yoga (est. 2003) and travels around the world teaching yoga, writing, meditation, and self-transformation.

Lowitz has published 20 books in many genres, most recently a YA novel, *Up from the Sea* (Crown/ Penguin Random House). Her awards include the APALA Award for Young Adult Literature, a PEN Fiction Award, the PEN Oakland Josephine Miles Poetry Award, grants from the National Endowment for the Arts, National Endowment for the Humanities, the California Arts Council, and the Japan-U.S. Friendship

Commission Prize in Translation from Columbia University. Her classic *Yoga Poems: Lines to Unfold By*, and its companion book: *Yoga Heart: Lines on the Six Perfections*, are popular among students of yoga and Buddhism worldwide. She has also published a best-selling memoir, *In Search of the Sun: One Woman's Quest to Find Family in Japan*, which Om Yoga's Cyndi Lee called "A love story and a yoga page-turner."

Lowitz's writing has appeared in the *New York Times, Shambhala Sun, The Huffington Post, Best Buddhist Writing, Yoga Journal, Yoga Journal Japan, Wanderlust, Elephant Journal, Origin, Mantra, Asana, Yoga International, The Manifest-Station* and others. Visit her at: www.lezalowitz.com or at her yoga studio: www.sunandmoon.jp

About the Illustrator

AMANDA GIACOMINI (aka 10,000 Buddhas) is an artist, yoga teacher and storyteller. Her 10,000 Buddhas project was inspired by a pilgrimage to the Ajanta caves in India where she saw a two thousand year old mural of a thousand Buddhas meditating together. This experience sparked an awakening, which led her on a mission to paint 10,000 Buddhas, spreading a message of kindness, compassion, and connection with her art. Over the course of a decade, Amanda reached and surpassed her goal, making 10,000 Buddhas a highly sought after, worldwide art project, including large scale public murals, fine art paintings, works on paper, and textiles. Her street art can be found across the United States and in Panama, Costa Rica, Germany and Japan.

Amanda has taught yoga to tens of thousands of people all over the world; from prestigious art museums and yoga festivals to The White House and the Forbidden City in China. She is the co-founder of Point Reyes Yoga, a studio she and her husband, MC YOGI, started in 2001. She has been featured on the cover of *Yoga Journal* and *Mantra Magazine* and inside many publications including *Yoga International, New York Yoga and Life, LA YOGA, Origin Magazine, Tricyle,* and *Lion's Roar.* Amanda lives in Northern California with her husband MC YOGI and continues to paint Buddhas.